Using Music to Foster Your Grandchild's Development

A Practical Guide for Grandparents

To Larry & Kim, with love, Mike

Michael Montague, PhD

Cosmic Music, LLC

Using Music to Foster Your Grandchild's Development
A Practical Guide for Grandparents
Michael Montague
Cosmic Music, LLC

Published by Cosmic Music, LLC, St. Louis, MO
Copyright ©2020 Michael Montague
All rights reserved.

No part of this publication may be reproduced, stored in a retrieval system, or transmitted in any form or by any means, electronic, mechanical, photocopying, recording, scanning, or otherwise, except as permitted under Section 107 or 108 of the 1976 United States Copyright Act, without the prior written permission of the Publisher. Requests to the Publisher for permission should be addressed to Permissions Department, Cosmic Music, LLC, info@cosmicmusicpro.com.

Limit of Liability/Disclaimer of Warranty: While the publisher and author have used their best efforts in preparing this book, they make no representations or warranties with respect to the accuracy or completeness of the contents of this book and specifically disclaim any implied warranties of merchantability or fitness for a particular purpose. No warranty may be created or extended by sales representatives or written sales materials. The advice and strategies contained herein may not be suitable for your situation. You should consult with a professional where appropriate. Neither the publisher nor author shall be liable for any loss of profit or any other commercial damages, including but not limited to special, incidental, consequential, or other damages.

Editor: Karen Tucker

Cover and Interior design: Davis Creative, DavisCreative.com

Illustrations: Peg McClure, PegsPortfolio.com

Library of Congress Cataloging-in-Publication Data

Library of Congress Control Number: 2020918820

Michael Montague

Using Music to Foster Your Grandchild's Development: A Practical Guide for Grandparents

ISBN: 978-1-7339169-3-6 (paperback)
      978-1-7339169-4-3 (hardback)
      978-1-7339169-5-0 (ebook)

Library of Congress subject headings:

1. MUS022000 MUSIC / Instruction & Study / General 2. EDU057000 EDUCATION / Arts in Education 3. FAM000000 FAMILY & RELATIONSHIPS / General

2020

ATTENTION CORPORATIONS, UNIVERSITIES, COLLEGES AND PROFESSIONAL ORGANIZATIONS: Quantity discounts are available on bulk purchases of this book for educational, gift purposes, or as premiums for increasing magazine subscriptions or renewals. Special books or book excerpts can also be created to fit specific needs. For information, please contact Cosmic Music, LLC, info@cosmicmusicpro.com.

I dedicate this book to the memory of my late Irish grandmother, Margaret O'Connor née Walsh, who gave me so much in life with her sense of humor, her ability to tell a good story, and most of all, her unconditional love.

Acknowledgments

First, I am grateful to Kenneth Webster, an accomplished educator, for his advice, encouragement, and unwavering love during the writing of this book.

I also thank Sharon Carter (Eichenberger) and Ike Eichenberger, two experienced music teachers and grandparents, for their critical reading of the manuscript.

I am grateful to Karen Tucker who edited the manuscript, thereby greatly improving it, and to Peg McClure for her fine illustrations.

Finally, I truly appreciate the many loving grandparents and their grandchildren whom I have known and observed over the course of a lifetime.

Table of Contents

Introduction 1

Grandparents Are Important 5
More Important Than We Think

How Our Grandchildren Learn 11
Grandparents Can Help—a Lot!

Music and Your Grandchild's Brain 19
A Primer for Grandparents

But I'm Not a Musician 27
You, as a Grandparent, Can Still Help Immensely

Music and Your Youngest Grandchildren 31
Birth through Age Two

Music in the First Years of School 37
Ages Three through Seven

Music in the Middle Years 49
Ages Eight through Twelve

Music in the Teen Years 55
Ages Thirteen through Eighteen

Quick Summary of Key Points 65

Appendix A: Musical Toys in the Early Years 67

Appendix B: Listening Activities for Young Ears 71

Further Reading 75

About the Author 77

Introduction

Several years ago, I enjoyed the great privilege of teaching a short course on music and science to a wonderful group of older professional people at Washington University in St. Louis. It was a delightful experience. I hope that my students learned something about the synergies between science and music, but regardless of any value of my instruction to them, I certainly learned something important *from* them. I learned how much grandparents genuinely want to be engaged completely and actively with the lives, play, learning, and passions of their grandchildren.

Perhaps half the members of my class were grandparents, and many took my course primarily because they wanted to learn more about music so that they could interact with their musical grandchildren. In some cases, their grandchildren were quite young, and my students wanted to engage in "musical play" with them. With older grandchildren, they wanted to have information about encouraging musical interest and training. In other words, they truly wanted to know what to *do* to help the children grow and develop their full potential as human beings.

As I later converted this university-level course into a full-length book, *The Science of Music and the Music of Science: How Music Reveals Our Brain, Our Humanity, and the Cosmos,* available for purchase on Amazon and elsewhere, I also reflected on the reasons that so many of my grandparent students were interested in learning about music and whether I could help them more directly. I began to think that many grandparents might be interested in a brief, accessible book that would provide practical suggestions on the ways that they could help their musical grandchildren.

This new book would not deal with the broad range of topics that I covered in *The Science of Music*. Rather, it would focus on **practical suggestions** for grandparents whose grandchildren were at various ages or stages of development, and who possessed different degrees of skill in music. In other words, it would be a handbook—a guide—rather than a textbook.

I also knew that many densely written, highly academic books on the market had reviewed the psychological literature on child development and some had even reviewed aspects of music education, training, and its value to the cognitive development of children. While these are valuable books indeed, they provide much more detailed information than the average grandparent would need or want.

This book aims to take the contemporary findings in the scientific literature on child development and music education and convert those findings into an accessible "airplane read" that is focused on the pragmatic—the really useful—aspects of that science. It is my profound hope that readers will finish this book with dozens of ideas for fostering the musical growth of their grandchildren and thereby connect even more profoundly with them on a human level. After all, isn't that one of the best aspects of living our lives?

Michael J. Montague, Ph.D.

Grandparents Are Important

More Important Than We Think

We live in a hectic, time-compressed world. Parents are besieged by demands coming from everywhere: work, children, spouse, social life, civic responsibilities, religious obligations, other family members, and on and on.

Of course, parents want only the best for their children. That's a given. But how to provide it?

That's where grandparents enter the picture. Grandparents are far more important than most people think because they can do so much to ensure the well-being and nurturing of their special contribution to the world, their own grandchildren.

Connection

Grandparents and grandchildren have a unique bond. For one thing, they have a common foe: **the parents**. By that, I'm being facetious, of course, though it is a statement with a kernel of frequently underappreciated truth. Parents must be disciplinarians and authority figures. It's part of their job. Also, parents are often so busy being parents that they can't be as connected, as fun-filled, as open to alternative experiences, as nonauthoritative, as relaxed, as "chilled," as stably present, or as spontaneous as grandparents can be. Children need such spontaneity. Indeed, they crave it.

Resources

Grandparents often have more free time than parents and, often, more resources too. These resources, of course, may include discretionary money to spend on grandchildren. Far more important, they include wisdom, understanding, knowledge in the ways of the world, and a firm conviction that life is to be lived in fifth gear—full out, fully engaged, with as much joy and love as they can possibly muster. Grandparents can give children the courage, the security, and the resources to do exactly that, thereby creating an enormously positive influence on their whole lives.

History

Grandparents are also teachers of their grandchildren. First off, they teach by example. They teach grandchildren what it means to be an older adult. Second, they often teach grandchildren many apparently small but nonetheless important facts about merely living in the world that parents have overlooked or don't have the time to teach. Such facts can range from how to use the rearview mirror of an automobile, how to bait a fishing hook, how to enjoy a musical comedy, how to build a bookshelf, how to prepare lasagna, or the complexities of a baseball game. Grandparents can fill these gaps.

One gap, of course, is detailed family history. Grandchildren often yearn to know, "Where did I come from?" Grandparents hold the keys to this historical information. As one personal example, I loved the stories of Ireland told to me by my own grandmother. She was born in County Waterford in southern Ireland and told stories of her own girlhood that mesmerized me as a child. Grandchildren gain greatly from knowing their "roots" and family background—information often supplied to them only by their grandparents. They also enjoy learning about the childhoods of their own parents, and in that regard, grandparents know the *real* story.

Unconditional Love

Oftentimes, grandchildren feel less judged by grandparents than by their own parents. They don't have to "live up to" some standard or other. They can be fully themselves, completely human, but also completely a child. They are loved unconditionally. What a wonderful gift for grandparents to give to their grandchildren! Often, only grandparents can give such a gift because, after all, the disciplinary role of a parent is different. Also, grandparents often possess the gift of patience, something that busy parents may struggle to maintain. This is patience born from experience because they've already been through the "parenting thing" and understand its pitfalls and potential mistakes too.

In this book, we'll specifically discuss the role of grandparents in the music education of their grandchildren. The gifts of music and music-making are of great value to children. In later chapters, we'll explore the reasons that music provides so much richness to our grandchildren. More important, we'll discuss many practical suggestions for giving this magnificent gift, even if you, as a grandparent, don't understand much about music-making yourself.

In fact, this book provides numerous practical, easily understood suggestions to grandparents of musical grandchildren, even if the grandparents lack musical understanding or musicianship when beginning this book. Everyone gains by the experience.

While musical experiences are immensely valuable in themselves, they also provide a vehicle for other interactions. Many times, grandparents will ask, "I'd like to do something new and different with my grandchild, but I'm running out of ideas." This book will supply numerous ideas as well as provide resources to find even more of them.

So, let's begin our exploration. This book is organized intuitively and need not be read linearly, that is, from chapter to chapter in succession. You can skip around if you choose to do so. We'll begin with the basics of how children learn through activities. Then, we'll discuss music through the various ages of development. In each case, I'll aim toward practical ideas and suggestions for activity-based learning. I'll also provide some information about music and your grandchild's developing brain. This is a topic that has received much attention lately. Finally, a summary in the last chapter will provide you, the reader, with a ready reference and reminder.

I sincerely hope that this short guide will be useful to you in building a superb relationship with your grandchildren. That's my ultimate goal, in part because your relationship helps to determine the future of the human race.

Grandparents Are Important

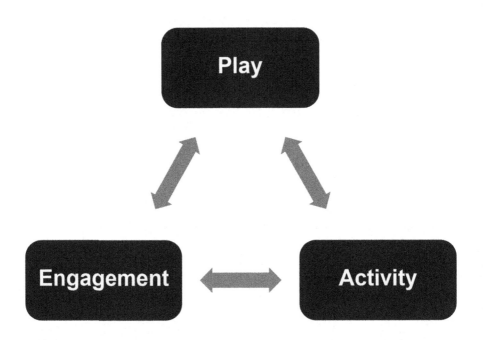

How Our Grandchildren Learn

Grandparents Can Help—a Lot!

Learning in childhood has been the subject of innumerable books, journal articles, and university courses. And no wonder. Between birth and age 18 or so, children must learn enough to survive in an increasingly complex, technically sophisticated world. This involves not only "book learning" but also all the elements of intellectual functioning, including emotional control, interpersonal skills, problem-solving abilities, and many other complex capabilities necessary in a mature, functioning adult. When stated in this way, it's amazing that the majority of children *do* succeed in learning enough to function rather well in the world.

The Brain Grows

Part of the reason that this learning is possible is through what neuroscientists call **neuroplasticity**. Everyone knows that plastics can be molded—formed into new shapes. It's like that with the child's brain. As children grow, their brains physically change in response to adapting to their environment. The brain is, therefore, plastic and changeable at the functional, structural, and microscopic levels *in response* to experiences, what the child learns, the demands placed upon his behavior by others, etc. Another way to express this idea is to say that new experiences actually catalyze (promote, create) the growth of the brain.

Perhaps you already know that the brain is the organ that matures and changes more than any other as your grandchild grows from infancy through adulthood. In fact, the brain continues to change significantly throughout a person's twenties and, to some extent, throughout all the adult years, though at a significantly slower pace in later life.

Without describing it in too much detail, the brain is composed of 100 billion **neurons**, or nerve cells. These connect to each other through **synapses**, which can be thought of in some ways as "electronic switches." Signals ("firings") from neurons are routed through these switches in complex ways. Learning apparently occurs when a particular switched route of signal transmission is used over and over again. If a route is not used, however, it may disappear altogether.

Stages for Learning

As children grow through the various stages of childhood, opportunities arise for learning specific skills and concepts easily and naturally. Once that stage passes, however, the skill may be much more difficult to acquire. Let's think about a couple of examples.

Anyone who has ever raised a puppy knows that it's much easier to teach certain behaviors to a seven-week-old puppy than to a two-year-old dog. For example, younger dogs can easily be introduced to strangers without being aggressive, but an older dog, never exposed to strangers, may never be cured of its innate aggression directed toward strange people. As another example, younger dogs can be shown that elevators are not to be feared, whereas an older dog, not exposed to elevators before, may be forever frightened of them.

Humans are very much like that. Children pass through stages when certain skills are easily acquired, but once that age has passed, the skill becomes far more difficult to learn. One common example used throughout the scientific literature is language acquisition. Children begin to learn language a few weeks before birth. The major window of time for language acquisition is between birth and about nine years of age. After that, children rarely learn to speak a new language without an accent unless they are already multilingual. Parents or grandparents who give their children or grandchildren the gift of a second or third language have helped those children immensely. Their brains actually become "wired"—meaning that the synapses work properly—for learning multiple languages much more easily.

New Experiences Enrich Your Grandchild

And so, what's the lesson about childhood learning here? It's simple. Grandparents can help their grandchildren to learn by giving them abundant, diverse, wonderful new experiences. Parents may not have the time or energy to be able to provide as many of these new experiences as the child can assimilate, but grandparents often do.

Just think for a moment of all the new experiences that are possible! Speaking, reading, singing, dancing, building, assembling, demonstrating, and on and on. Each one of these experiences causes neurons to "fire" and synapses to form within your grandchild's amazing, growing, developing brain. As a grandparent, you can enrich the child's environment in a unique way—a way that arises only through your personal relationship with your grandchild.

While this book deals primarily with musical enrichment and its importance for brain development, you, as a grandparent, can provide numerous valuable experiences to your grandchild. Being aware that children have windows of opportunity is important so that you don't miss an opportunity when it arises.

Let Your Grandchild Show Readiness

What else do scientists emphasize when they discuss childhood learning? One finding seems significant. Let your grandchild help lead the way. While you can provide the new experiences, allow your grandchild to let you know whether she is ready for it and really interested in it. Do not try to force the experience on the child but, rather, merely make the experience available. The concept here is to expose your grandchild to an experience. Then take the child's cue on her readiness.

Child's Play—Make It All a Game!

Often one of the best ways to help a child is to make a game of the learning process. After all, the job of the child is to play. The more playful the learning experience becomes, particularly in early childhood, the greater the level of enjoyment of the child. The more enjoyment, the more motivation to learn. And the more learning, the greater the enjoyment. This process becomes a self-reinforcing loop. In other words, make it fun—both for you and the child!

Another principle of learning culled from the scientific literature is the concept of age-appropriate activities. Most grandparents understand this intuitively, but sometimes parents and grandparents may "push too hard" for the child's level of readiness. Remember those stages of receptiveness that we discussed above. If a child doesn't have the muscular coordination necessary for the learning activity, for example, the activity won't be effective even if the child's brain may be ready. Learning is a body-brain process. It doesn't occur solely in the brain.

Activities and Engagement

Note that we're emphasizing **activity** here. The best learning experiences almost always involve an activity, with emphasis here on the root of the word: *active*. This is often physical activity, of course, but not necessarily. In other words, don't just *tell* your grandchild about something. Demonstrate it. Act it out. Engage the child with you. The neurons in the child's brain will begin to fire on all cylinders.

One way to be active in the learning process is to ask questions. Here's an example. Let's say that you're reading a beautifully illustrated book to your three-year-old grandchild. As you read, ask questions such as:
- "What color do you like most in this picture?"
- "What do you think is going to happen next in the story?"
- "What do you like most about this character?"
- "Why do you think this character acted that way?"

This engages your grandchild, connects the two of you, and demonstrates that you really want to know what your grandchild thinks. This, in turn, makes the child feel valued and loved.

KEY POINTS

- Your grandchild's brain is plastic. It changes constantly in ways related to learning.
- Developmental stages in your grandchild's life create windows during which it's much easier to learn certain skills, such as language.
- Grandparents have a wonderful opportunity to provide learning experiences to their grandchildren.
- Because a child's job is to play, the more that you can make learning be like play, the better for everyone. Let your grandchild lead the way most of the time.
- A key to learning is to make it active, engaging as many senses and as much of the child's being as possible.
- Active learning often involves asking your grandchildren questions about how they feel during the experience.

How Our Grandchildren Learn

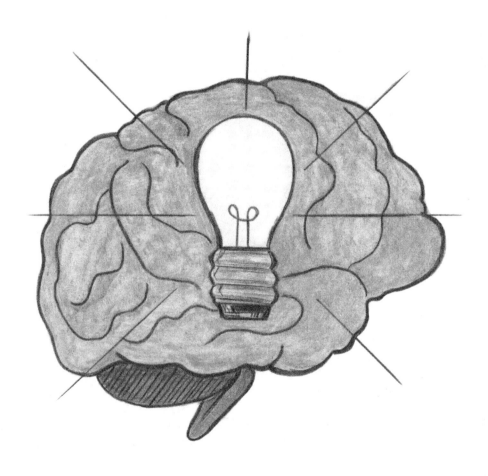

Music and Your Grandchild's Brain

A Primer for Grandparents

It's obvious that the brain and the rest of the nervous system are extraordinarily complex. We've already discovered that the brain is composed of 100 billion neurons (nerve cells) connected together in vast and complex arrays through "electronic switches" called synapses. And we've learned that the wiring of the brain is plastic, changing during the development of your grandchild and influenced by every one of her experiences in life.

Innumerable academic texts have been written about every aspect of this wonderful and amazing nervous system. In the last 25 years, however, neuroscientists have made even more rapid progress because they can now use special tools to obtain images of *living* human brains as their owners are thinking thoughts or while they engage in complex tasks. This is quite a stunning advance.

Music as a Powerful Tool to Understand the Brain

In using these imaging tools, neuroscientists often ask a person to listen to music or even perform music to find out exactly how the brain works. Perhaps surprisingly, music is an especially useful probe into the inner workings of our nervous systems. A person can be placed in an imaging machine, such as a functional MRI (magnetic resonance imager) or PET (positron-emission tomography) scanner, and then asked to listen to various kinds of music, to perform music, or even to compose music. The results of the imaging allow neuroscientists to find out which areas of the brain are involved in performing each task.

Unlike most other experimental conditions, neuroscientists have found that making music involves almost *every* part of the brain working together. The performance of most other tasks, such as reading or drawing, requires the activities of only a few brain sectors. Not so with music. With music, almost the whole brain "lights up"—a phrase used by neuroscientists as they observe brain activity in specific areas of the brain image.

Over the course of this book, we'll mention the idea repeatedly that music involves the brain in a global sense as well as how this observation helps us to think about childhood learning. In a simple sense, however, making music or participating in music is likely to involve those areas of the brain devoted to hearing, sound comprehension and organization, motor control, pleasure perception, planning, coordination, and timekeeping (rhythm). Brain areas devoted to those functions are scattered throughout the brain and act coordinately and either simultaneously or sequentially to allow the creation of music.

In the previous chapter, we pointed out that the process of learning stimulates the development of the brain. Might it be that the tremendous demands placed on the brain by music-making stimulate brain development to an especially high level? That's an interesting idea, of course, but we'd need a lot of good evidence to be confident of such a conclusion.

Music and Academic Achievement

In fact, much evidence does exist that participation in music education correlates with high-level performance in other academic pursuits. These studies have primarily been done retrospectively, however. In other words, music students are compared with those not studying music. Such research is fraught with the potential to derive erroneous conclusions. For example, it may be that music students happen to come from wealthier families that value overall education more. It may be that music students are more highly motivated, or more disciplined, or more anxious to please adults, or lack athletic prowess and therefore gravitate to music, or possess personality characteristics related somehow to music that also, incidentally, influence academic performance.

The only studies that would be convincing about the power of music education would be randomized, prospective, controlled studies. In that type of study, the investigator would select a group of children, perhaps from a below-average socioeconomic group, and then divide the group into three sectors (called **arms** of the study). One subgroup of children would be given no special intervention at all. The second would receive long-term music education. The third would receive some other unrelated intervention, for example, soccer coaching, art classes, or exposure to the dramatic arts. The children in each group would be followed, preferably for years, and their abilities, skills, and achievements monitored across a wide range of areas.

If the group of children with the music training demonstrated superior academic skill or achievement in one or more areas, that would indicate that music training produced effects beyond those effects that would be expected solely from exposure to music. On the other hand, if no such effect were noted, we'd conclude that training in music was good for the children because it made them more musical, but that we could not conclude that they improved in other areas as well.

Controlled Experimental Study

One of the best of these studies is being carried out by Dr. Assal Habibi of the Brain and Creativity Institute of the University of Southern California. She chose 80 children between the ages of and six and seven from an economically underprivileged part of Los Angeles. These 80 children were divided into three groups. One group was randomly assigned to study music, a second was enrolled in a soccer program, and the third received only the usual high-quality academic instruction. The children are being tested every year to measure memory, language, music and speech processing, and brain development. Of course, the evaluation of these three groups of children showed no differences between the children at the *beginning* of the study.

After two years, many differences emerged between the three groups of children. One major finding was that the music-trained children were able to process sound, including melody, language, and pitch, significantly faster than the other children. In addition, Dr. Habibi has found actual structural differences in the **temporal lobes** (the sound-processing part of the brain). This difference demonstrated greater brain maturation. Finally, the right and left parts of the brains of musically trained children were connected by a larger "cable," something called the **corpus callosum**. The main conclusion of all these findings so far is that training in music enhances language and actually alters brain structure compared with the two control groups. After four years of the study, Dr. Habibi reports that children given music training also showed greater emotional stability and less hyperactivity and aggression.

Other Conclusions:
Music Is Good for Your Grandchild's Brain!

Although often employing less rigorous experimental conditions, other investigators have consistently concluded that children given musical training do better in school in a variety of subjects. Apparently, the combination of discipline, interest, and ability required to pursue musical activities correlates with success in a variety of academic disciplines. For example, one consistent finding is an improvement in those academic subjects that require auditory processing, including the language arts. This is not unexpected because the areas of the brain that handle language are closely aligned with those that handle musicality.

Language is, of course, a key to academic performance. Without good language skills, children are at a decided disadvantage. This alone could account for the significant positive correlation between general academic performance and music education.

A fairly safe conclusion based on all the scientific results available to us is that music is good for your grandchild's brain development! It helps especially with language and general auditory processing but may well accelerate overall brain development and maturation as well as facilitate the connection between the left and right brains. That's pretty exciting and provides more than sufficient justification for you, as a grandparent, to help expose your grandchildren to music education.

Music Is More Than a Means to an End

As if improved academic performance weren't sufficient justification for music education, there's more—much more.

When you, as a grandparent, give your grandchild the gift of music, you are giving the gift of lifelong pleasure. Music becomes part of the fabric of your grandchild's personality and provides a valued life skill. It also helps significantly with socialization because music is almost always a group enterprise. Your grandchild can make music with other musicians or other people can listen as the child makes music. Therefore, music training is likely to improve interpersonal relationships and provide the pleasure of companionship and shared interest, as well as a sense of skill and accomplishment.

In other words, music training enhances the fundamental humanity of your grandchild. It helps children of all ages to express themselves at the deepest levels of experience. Like the other humanities, including literature, history, drama, the visual arts, and dance, music makes us more human and, hopefully, more humane.

The emphasis today in our school systems is often on STEM: science + technology + engineering + mathematics. We live in a technically complex world, and these subjects are critically important, especially vocationally. I think, however, that we should emphasize STEAM rather than merely STEM. The "A" stands for all the arts and humanities. The humanities provide your grandchild with the experiences necessary to become fully human, fully alive, and fully engaged with the world and add joy to the experience of living. You, as a grandparent, can help provide this gift to your grandchild. It's a gift that truly keeps on giving—for a lifetime!

KEY POINTS

- We can now take pictures of our complex brains as they are engaged in specific tasks.
- When we take these pictures of the brain as their owners make music, nearly the entire brain "lights up," that is, we can see activity throughout almost the entire brain. This is probably because music is so demanding, involving motor control, pleasure perception, sound processing, sound interpretation, planning, evaluation, judgment, time perception, and many other complex tasks.
- Much evidence shows that those students who perform music are likely to do better academically.
- The best controlled, prospective studies show that students given music education show more rapid maturation of their brains and better language processing.
- Music is good for the brain development of your grandchildren based on everything that scientists have found about human behavior.
- Music training is more than a means to an academic end, however. It makes us more human and is, therefore, a tremendous gift that you, as a grandparent, can help give to your grandchild.

But I'm Not a Musician

*You, as a Grandparent,
Can Still Help Immensely*

In listening to the concerns of grandparents as they think about enriching the lives of their grandchildren with music, I frequently hear concerns expressed in words like the following:

"I'm not a musical person. How can I help my young grandchild appreciate music?"

"I don't play a musical instrument and know nothing about it. How can I even discuss these things with my musical grandchildren?"

"I know nothing about how my grandchild learns music. How can I possibly help?"

My answer to these and similar questions is simply: *Don't worry!*

First off, with few exceptions, all human beings are musical. Musicality seems fundamental to our nature, to the essence of being human. Evolutionary biologists continue to try to explain how music is found in all human cultures, and frankly, we still don't understand its origins very well. But we do know, for certain, that humans are musical. And it's extremely likely that both you and your grandchild are musical—because you're both human beings!

Second, it's not up to you, as a grandparent, to teach complex musical concepts to your grandchildren. Your task is much simpler. Your task, when the child is young, is to make simple music with your grandchild, and when the child is older, to expedite or facilitate music education. That's it. And this book is designed to help you do just that.

Third, both you and your grandchild will benefit enormously from even the most minimal involvement in music education. You will become even more closely bonded together. This book is designed to give you many ideas for this bonding process derived from music-making. With this guide in your hand, you're not alone in trying to enrich the life of your grandchild.

In other words, regardless of your level of musical training or skill, you are *ideally suited* to bring the richness of music to your grandchildren, and this guide will help you do it.

But I'm Not a Musician

Music and Your Youngest Grandchildren

Birth through Age Two

Infancy is a time of rapid brain growth and development. Your grandchild is learning and growing at an extraordinary pace. Near the end of this stage, of course, your grandchild, now a toddler, has developed some language proficiency, and it becomes easier to be interactive. But you may be surprised at the learning games that are possible even with the youngest infant.

First off, let's consider singing to your grandchild. For grandparents who immediately say, "I'm not a singer and can't carry a tune in a bucket," I say, "Forget about it!" You don't have to be a fine singer to bond vocally with your grandchild, just like you don't have to be an eloquent speaker to communicate. The value is in the interaction between you and your grandchild.

Sing

Many scientists who study the origin of musicality in humans think that it may well have originated in lullabies—the cooing and soft vocalizations made by mothers (and fathers) to their infant children. I profoundly wish that every child could enjoy the gift that my own mother gave to me—she sang to me routinely as she held me close and comforted me. Grandparents can do the same thing, and their songs are an equally valuable gift to grandchildren.

Singing exposes the growing infant brain to sound like no other. It is a warm, caring sound in infancy—comforting—yet it also stimulates the growing brain of the infant and helps on the path to more mature language development.

Bottom line: Sing to your grandchild at every opportunity—and that goes for grandfathers as much as grandmothers!

Explore All Sorts of Sounds to Stimulate Your Grandchild

Infants are exploring the world of sound in many other ways as well. They deliberately drop objects, for example, and take delight in the sound that is generated. As they develop motor control, they begin to bang on objects and seem to delight in their growing ability to control their environment to make various sounds. While perhaps not "musical," these sounds are the prelude to music-making, auditory development, and the concept of cause and effect.

As a grandparent, you can bang on anything and observe your grandchild's response. What a wonderful game! As the child grows, you can help your grandchild do the banging. Whether it's on pots and pans or a toy piano, the child begins to learn concepts of sound generation.

The game of hand clapping is also a terrific engagement activity later in this period of development. Clap out a simple rhythm and see if your grandchild can imitate the rhythm. Alternatively, listen to a pattern of sound that your grandchild is making and mimic it. Reproducing the sounds of your grandchild is a wonderful way to connect and engage.

Fill Your Home with Music

As part of this general exposure to sound, fill your home with music of all kinds. Early on, it may seem that your grandchild is largely ignoring this music, but that's not the case. The music is penetrating the child's developing brain, influencing auditory pathways, and helping the child learn the language of various kinds of music. Remember that music is a type of language, and just as your grandchild is learning a native language—and hopefully you're teaching another language too—your grandchild can begin to learn the language of music as well.

Dance—As If Future Motor Control Depends on It

As motor development reaches a much higher level late in this early period of child development, your grandchild not only begins to walk but can dance as well. Yes, **dance**! The dance moves may be uncoordinated, but you can dance to music with your grandchild, even if it's only the simplest of steps or movements. This begins to teach the relationship between movement and rhythm, a valuable concept for motor development in general. And what a wonderful game dancing becomes! Imagine what your grandchild begins to "think" having fun with you by dancing and moving to music! Both you and your grandchild will be delighted.

Using Music to Foster Your Grandchild's Development

KEY POINTS

- The brain is developing at an enormous rate during this early stage of child development. New synapses are being laid down. Neurons are increasing in number.
- Lullabies seem linked to the development of language, both in the child and in our whole human race.
- Sing to your grandchild! You don't have to be a great singer. It doesn't matter. Never be embarrassed about your own musical ability. Enjoy it!
- Explore all kinds of sounds with your grandchild as a game. Drop things on the floor or on a table. Strike things. Let the child mimic you and you mimic the child. Share in the delight as your grandchild discovers how sounds can be made and the great variety of sounds that are possible. (See Appendices A and B for many specific suggestions.)
- Fill your home with all kinds of music. This will help your grandchild learn the multiple dialects of music, including music from a variety of cultures.
- Dance to music with your grandchild. You can sing as you dance or dance to recorded music. But dance! Dancing is a wonderful game that engages all the senses of your grandchild and provides intense joy and connection.

Music and Your Youngest Grandchildren

Music in the First Years of School

Ages Three through Seven

By age three and certainly by age four, many children are ready to begin a much more defined education in music. Part of the reason for this is that children have usually acquired a significant facility with language and that enables teaching and engagement with them at a far more sophisticated level of interaction.

Continue with Singing and Dancing

Even so, many of the same activities described in the previous chapter continue to be useful. Singing, dancing, listening (now at a more sophisticated level), and sound-generating toys of all kinds still apply.

Don't be surprised if your grandchild begins to express preferences about which types of music she likes. That's fine, of course, but make certain that you continue to expose your grandchild to other musical forms as well. Some adults would argue that only classical music is "good" music for kids. Not so, in my estimation. "Good" music comes to us in many genres, and the exclusion of any of them excludes valuable experiences that you could be giving your grandchild.

Dancing can also be more sophisticated than earlier in life. Ask questions:

- "What does happy dancing look like to you?"
- "What does sad dancing sound look like?"
- "How do you dance to happy or sad music?"

On your CD player or other device, play some selections from different types of music and ask, "Would this music cause you to be sad or happy when you dance to it?"

Today, we have YouTube and other music streaming services, making the types of music available to us virtually limitless. After playing three distinct pieces, you might ask:
- "Which of these three musical pieces is your favorite? Why?"
- "How does it make you feel?"

Perhaps even more important than exposing your grandchild to recorded music is exposure to **live music** of all kinds. Take your grandchild to a musical, for example. What an exciting adventure! Any kind of outdoor concert is terrific as well. Perhaps your local fair has a group of live musicians. Take your grandchild up to the musicians between sets and have the musicians introduce themselves and their instruments. In my own experience during 50 adult years of performing music, I have *never* seen one of my fellow musicians fail to be delighted to talk to a young child about musical instruments and about music-making.

Describing and Naming Sounds

At some point during this developmental period, often quite early, your grandchild will be ready to put names to specific sounds. In the same manner that the child becomes ready to name visual sensations, such as colors, the child becomes able to name sounds and to describe them as well.

To develop this new ability, you may want to play games such as:
- "Which sound is louder?"
- "Which sound is softer?"
- "Can you sing that sound?" (That is, can you match the pitch of the sound?)

At some point, you could ask, "Which sound is lower?" or "Which sound is higher?" These kinds of interactive questions help to develop the connection between your grandchild's ear, the sound processing in the brain, and the part of the brain that classifies and groups sensations.

This may be the appropriate time also to purchase recordings of specific musical instruments and a picture book of those instruments. Your grandchild may be able, when ready (remember the concept of readiness discussed before), to connect the sound of a bassoon or a violin with the picture of that instrument, after you've had the pleasure of teaching about the instruments. A picture book works well, but cards with pictures of the instruments can also be useful. This is quite a complex task, but many children will be ready by four to six years of age, at about the start of kindergarten or first grade.

While these questions and activities are powerful games to promote those brain circuits dealing with sound discrimination, always remember that it's all just a game! You, as the grandparent, will do some teaching or demonstration, but the fun of the game is when your grandchild makes the identification. Be prepared to praise but never look disappointed in an "incorrect" answer.

Often, the best praise is not "You got that one right!" but rather, "You really put a lot of effort and thinking into that question!"

Learning Games Are NOT about Getting the Right Answer—They Must Be FUN!

This is actually an important point for all of these games. Don't get hung up on the right answer. It's about the process of learning and the joy of acquiring new knowledge and skill. As a grandparent, in contrast to a paid tutor or even a parent, you are in a special position to give the pleasure of learning to your grandchild nonjudgmentally. Who cares whether the child mixes up a violin with a bassoon sound? What does it matter? In the end, it's the fun of guessing and learning with you guiding the way because you're interested enough in *your grandchild* to spend the time teaching and the two of you learning together.

This Is the Window of Time to Teach Absolute Pitch

Some children are born with something called **absolute pitch**, also referred to as **perfect pitch**. These children can name a note when they hear it played, for example, on the piano, once they are taught the name of the note (the names of the pitches on the piano's black and white keys.) Absolute pitch can be quite valuable, especially for a musician, but interestingly, most musicians actually have **relative pitch** instead. With relative pitch, a musician can figure out the sound of any note once a known pitch is sounded with a pitch pipe or other instrument.

In theory, almost any child can be taught absolute pitch by a patient adult. All you need to do, as that very patient adult, is to sit at the piano, play an "A" or other note, tell your grandchild that it's an "A," and then have the child turn away as you play the note again, asking for the name of the note. This is entirely analogous to learning the names of colors, where the teaching adult names the color and asks the child its name until the child associates the color with the word that identifies it.

This naming of pitches is a wonderful game, just as the naming of colors in a drawing is a great game to be played by grandparent and grandchild. Absolute pitch is a lifelong gift to your grandchild, if you decide that it's worth your effort and if the child seems willing, capable, and patient enough to play the game.

As Your Grandchild Starts Formal Schooling

Many changes are in store for your grandchild with the advent of formal schooling. In this book, I'm going to discuss what would happen in a first-rate music program in a first-rate school system. Unfortunately, oftentimes, the school system is not first-rate and does not recognize the importance of the fine arts and the humanities. As previously mentioned, the school board may emphasize STEM rather than STEAM. That's a shame. Actually, it's a tragedy for the children.

You, as a grandparent, can do a lot if you don't think your grandchild is receiving the best education. You can appeal directly to the school board. You can run for a position on the school board. You can help to secure donations to buttress the fine arts program in the school. And, of course, you can, and should, complain loudly to everyone with any power to make a change.

But let's say that the school system is a good one, with good teachers, a balanced curriculum, and sufficient funds for both

STEM courses and the humanities and fine arts. What happens as your grandchild enters kindergarten?

A good kindergarten class emphasizes structured play, and part of that play is music-making. Even if the kindergarten teacher is not a pianist, much can be learned by group singing of simple songs, using simple musical toys such as a xylophone-like toy, or clapping rhythms together as dictated by the teacher or a member of the class. In the early grades, teachers will sometimes trade off responsibilities so that a more musically gifted teacher will provide music instruction to more than one classroom. Later on, good school systems will have a dedicated music teacher.

Music as an Extracurricular Activity

Regardless of the school system's attention to music, you, as a grandparent, can facilitate more musical experiences *outside* of the classroom. Dance classes or children's choirs (for example, at church) are always options, but there are other possibilities as well.

Much instrumental music can be an impossible challenge for children in this age range simply because of their small body size. Most wind instruments are simply too large for them to handle yet, as are most percussion instruments. Children in this age group can begin formal lessons on violin or piano, however. Each instrument has its advantages and disadvantages. Violins can be sized as half-, quarter-, or even eighth-sized instruments to fit small arms and hands. A string instrument like the violin helps your grandchild develop a sense of pitch in a powerful way. Unfortunately, the first sounds from the violin may not be very pleasant. In contrast, the piano provides a fixed pitch, and the sound will be pleasant as long as your grandchild depresses the correct key. But because the pitch is fixed, the child won't have the opportunity to develop a sense of pitch nearly as well as if your grandchild studied violin.

Bottom line: Either the correct-sized violin or a keyboard of some sort is effective to begin extracurricular music instruction with an actual musical instrument. It doesn't really matter whether your grandchild goes on with that first instrument. Your grandchild will learn the fundamentals of making music. And you'll be very proud!

Choosing a Music Teacher for Very Young Children

Selecting a music teacher is both challenging and important. If your grandchild wants to play violin, one of the best ways to start is with the Suzuki or other similar method of group instruction. Talk to other grandparents, music teachers, your grandchild's teachers, the local community music school, neighbors, and musical friends for recommendations. Personal recommendations are often the best way to evaluate teachers.

The same principles apply to piano instruction except that such instruction is usually individual, even at the beginner's level. Often, you will find many piano teachers available. Unfortunately, the best ones may have a waiting list. Be sure to select a piano teacher who has a good reputation for helping relatively young beginning students and who clearly understands their particular requirements. That means that you won't want to choose a frustrated piano virtuoso with a degree from Juilliard, but rather a kind, caring, empathic person who enjoys working with younger children.

Here are some of the ways that you as a grandparent can help most with this early music instruction:

1. Provide the financial resources necessary;
2. Transport your grandchild to the music lesson;
3. Sit quietly and unobtrusively through the lesson to offer encouragement and to observe the teacher at work;
4. Attend every recital or other public performance of your grandchild;
5. Ask questions, perhaps when driving home from the lesson: "What did you enjoy most about today's lesson?" or "What piece seems most difficult for you?" or "Is there some popular tune that you'd really like to learn to play?"

Music in the Early Elementary Years at School

In the first grades of elementary school, children acquire something important for further musical education, namely, the concept of written language. Much of the music-making that they are likely to do later in life will depend on being able to read standard Western musical notation. The concepts of reading notation are not that different from the fundamental concepts of written language. Both use symbols that are translated in time to sounds. Both rely on the ability of the brain to convert a visual perception of written symbols into a motor action of the body and to do this rapidly and, ultimately, almost effortlessly as the synapses (electronic switches) in your grandchild's brain become turned on sequentially in the right way. Reading words on paper and reading music symbols are both fun!

In the best school systems, the music teacher will begin to teach a bit about music notation to young students. But more advanced instruction isn't likely to occur in the school system until later grades.

That's where extracurricular music instruction, facilitated by you as a grandparent, can be so helpful. It gives your grandchild a head start for the next period of in-school music instruction when the child will begin to learn the details of Western music notation and develop a more refined ear.

KEY POINTS

- The musical activities developed earlier, such as singing and dancing, with your grandchild extend into this period of childhood development, though at a more sophisticated level as the child gains greater motor control.
- Continue to fill your grandchild's environment with all sorts of music and begin to ask how the child feels and/or reacts to various tunes that you play from CDs, YouTube, etc.
- Be sure to take your grandchild to live music at every opportunity, and don't ever hesitate to approach and speak with the musicians.
- With the advent of greater verbal ability, your grandchild will be able to name sounds. Try the game of matching various instrumental sounds to the pictures of the instruments. Try asking your grandchild to describe sounds as "high" or "low" or as "soft" or "loud." Again, the emphasis is NOT on the right answer but on having fun!
- This is the window of opportunity to teach absolute pitch to your grandchild, if you have the patience and the child has the inclination. The possession of absolute pitch is not

necessary to become an excellent musician, but it can be helpful, and it develops your grandchild's perception of sound in a wonderful way.
- The best school systems will emphasize and support the humanities and the fine arts. If you don't think that your grandchild's school system is sufficiently supportive, you can change it with determination. Talk to the school board.
- Extracurricular music education is extremely valuable for your grandchild. Young children are best suited to starting with either the violin or the piano. You can make this extracurricular instruction possible, thereby giving your grandchild an enormously valuable gift.
- The elementary years introduce your grandchild to reading and writing language, which has many similarities to reading and writing Western musical notation.

Music in the Middle Years

Ages Eight through Twelve

In many respects, these middle years of childhood are the most fun for you as a grandparent. Your grandchild is developing full verbal fluency, is able to read and write, is intensely curious about the world, and still very much wants to spend time with you. Of course, your grandchild is achieving more autonomy at the same time.

At this point, of course, your grandchild is developing a plethora of interests, some of which may not have anything to do with music at all. That's fine. Remember that your job as a grandparent is to facilitate experiences. If your grandchild begins to take a strong interest in science rather than in any of the arts, so be it. With any luck, though, you may be able to help your grandchild understand that interests are not either/or but rather both/and. This may not be an easy concept, but it's an important idea to ensure that your grandchild explores the world's many aspects.

Music in the School System in Third through Sixth Grades

In the best school systems, your grandchild will now begin to receive more formal musical instruction. Not only will children participate in dramatic plays that will probably include singing, but your grandchild may begin to receive exposure to musical instruments of various kinds.

For example, my first wind instrument was the Tonette, an inexpensive, indestructible song flute well suited to elementary music education. My music teacher used this easily played flute to teach the fundamentals of Western musical notation and to give the class an opportunity to make music as a group using a real musical instrument. That was an ear-opening and mind-opening experience for me.

Of course, if in your role as grandparent, you've already provided extracurricular musical training to your grandchild, some of this school exposure will be review. But that's fine. Your grandchild will be exposed to the concepts in a new and different way in the school setting.

It is also at this stage, with new exposures at school, that your grandchild may develop a "wandering eye" about which instrument to play. A good school system will have a day in which children are introduced to a wide variety of string, woodwind, brass, and percussion instruments under the observation of an experienced music teacher who will evaluate any natural tendencies of the child. For example, a child with a "good ear," that is, a good sense of pitch, may be well suited to a string instrument, a trombone, or a French horn, all of which require a strong sense of pitch discrimination. A highly intelligent child may be suited to a difficult instrument such as the clarinet. A strong-willed child, who seems to know no fear about anything, may be suited to the trumpet, which is one of the loudest and most penetrating of any instrument in the band or orchestra. A child with excellent mathematical concepts and a superior sense of rhythm may be ideally suited to the percussion family of instruments. A child who has already been studying violin or other string instrument may elect to continue.

Regardless of the child's innate abilities or proclivities, you, as a grandparent, can provide guidance, advice, and input to help your grandchild make the decision. No decision of this kind is irrevocable, however. Decisions can always be changed, but your grandchild ought to be given some autonomy in making this kind of decision.

Good school systems will begin to provide private or class instruction to instrumental music students. Most often, the child is taken out of class for 45 minutes to be given this special instruction. Some students may worry about their academic performance as a result of being absent from class, but as a grandparent, reassure them that it's fine and that the benefits to them will be significant.

To Rent or Buy a Musical Instrument for Your Grandchild?

Once your grandchild has decided which instrument to learn, you, as a grandparent, along with the parents, will be faced with the decision about whether to buy an instrument or to lease one for the school year. In general, leasing is best at first, especially with an option to purchase.

Leasing allows your grandchild to try out a choice and see if it's really suitable, all with minimal financial investment on your part. If your grandchild does fall in love with the flute or clarinet or trumpet, great! If it's not quite right, the choice is easily altered.

Ultimately, the successful choice of an instrument is based on several factors: (1) your grandchild's interests, (2) your grandchild's innate abilities or disabilities, and (3) the number of players needed in various musical groups. What is meant by (3) is that some instruments, like clarinets and flutes, will always be needed in abundance in bands, whereas others, like alto saxophones, will be needed in fewer numbers. But the single most important factor is (1), your grandchild's musical interests.

Bottom line: Don't sweat the decision. As long as you lease the instrument, your grandchild can always change, having at least several years to do so.

Music Theory and Music Appreciation: Constant Exposure to Music

A good school system will also teach your grandchild about both the theory of music and the appreciation of music, including aspects of music history. These are more likely to be part of the curriculum toward the end of this stage, that is, at about 11 or 12 years old and beyond.

Theory, history, and music appreciation are vital components of a good education in the fine arts, regardless of whether your grandchild goes on to play an instrument. Make certain that this is part of the curriculum. Again, you can help by constantly taking your grandchild to concerts and other live musical performances, including theatre and dance. You, as a grandparent, can easily be a part of your grandchild's appreciation of music. For grandparents looking for something to do with their grandchild, what could be better than taking the child to a symphony concert, the performance of a musical, or a band concert?

Taking your grandchild to a high school band or orchestra concert or a vocal music performance is especially worthwhile at this age. Afterward, be sure to ask questions like the following:

- "What did you enjoy most?"

- "What seemed most difficult to perform?"
- "Did you notice the clarinet solo in the second piece?"

Most important, point out that in a few years, your grandchild could be up on the stage, performing like those high school students!

KEY POINTS

- This is the period of childhood when your grandchildren are developing a plethora of interests. Let them! Promote them! Encourage them!
- This is also the period when school systems usually begin to teach music in a more formal way and to provide the opportunity to learn specific instruments.
- If possible, join your grandchild on "music day" when children are given the opportunity to try out various instruments to see what appeals to them. Always remember that this decision is not irrevocable.
- In general, leasing is more cost effective and more flexible than buying an instrument, even if you can afford to buy "the very best." If your grandchild does continue with the first choice in an instrument, by all means, purchase an excellent instrument, but there's no need initially.
- Make certain that your grandchild receives instruction in music theory and history. You can help with this instruction a great deal by taking your grandchild to various musical performances such as musical plays, vocal concerts, and high school band and orchestra concerts. It's helpful for you to point out that your 11- or 12-year-old grandchild could be making music like that in a few years.

Music in the Teen Years

Ages Thirteen through Eighteen

Now, the fun of music-making really begins for your grandchild!

Entering the teen years, the child has had several years of musical training on one or more instruments, or on voice, and is ready to become part of a performing ensemble of peers. Not only will the child advance musically in this new environment but also will advance socially because learning to make music is a group enterprise and requires a whole new set of skills for teamwork.

Grandparents who haven't participated in music as they were growing up may be mystified by the numbers and types of musical groups that are formed in the school. The names of these groups may seem strange. For that reason, here are some clarifications about these various musical ensembles (the word that we use to describe a group of musicians performing together). Please note that I'm focusing on those groups found in the school system rather than on rock groups, garage bands, or similar musical situations. All of those can be fun and valuable as well, but grandparents are more often concerned with school programs.

Types of Musical Ensembles for Your Grandchild

First off, there is a basic division between vocal and instrumental music.

Vocal Music

- Concert choir (male and female voices performing a wide variety of vocal music)
- Glee club (male and female voices performing popular music)
- Show choir (male and female voices performing show tunes, often with choreography)
- Girls' or boys' chorus (single-sex vocal groups)

Instrumental Music
Bands:

- Symphonic band (large wind band; no strings except perhaps double bass; huge sound)
- Concert band (no stringed instruments except double bass; performs concert band repertoire)
- Jazz band (no stringed instruments except double bass; performs jazz; smaller than concert band)
- Stage (pep) band (no stringed instruments except double bass; performs for sporting events; smaller than concert band; emphasizes saxophones, brass, and percussion)
- Marching band (performs for athletic events; no stringed instruments)

Orchestras:

- String orchestra (only stringed instruments)
- Full orchestra (stringed instruments plus woodwinds, brass, and percussion)
- Theater pit orchestra (plays for musical productions)

Small Ensembles:

- String quartet (two violins, viola, cello)

- Woodwind quintet (flute, clarinet, oboe, French horn, bassoon)
- Brass quintet (two trumpets, French horn, baritone, tuba)

Your grandchild may want to perform with one or more of these groups. Obviously, for children who play violin, they won't perform with any of the bands, but for those who play clarinet or saxophone, they may perform with several of them. Many musically talented teenagers perform in both a vocal and an instrumental group, and sometimes on multiple instruments.

Practicing

Bottom line: Practicing is essential. I'll write it again: *Practicing is essential.*

Often, children think that because professional music performance sounds so effortless, it must be effortless. It's not. A professional performer will have practiced many tens of thousands of hours.

Practicing is an art itself, and therefore, it need not be boring. After all, your grandchild will be making music when practicing. Some suggestions for you and your grandchild for successful practicing:

1. Have a good, quiet, dedicated space in the home to practice.
2. With your grandchild's private teacher as a guide, practice a combination of exercises, familiar material, and new material. The private teacher will help your grandchild set goals for each practice session, weekly goals, etc.
3. Practice SLOWLY at first. This is really important.

4. Practice regularly but don't become exhausted by the practice session.
5. Never practice errors. The synapses in your grandchild's brain will get "locked into" the error. Slow down and practice the passage correctly until it's right.
6. As a grandparent, be supportive and realistic about the necessity of practice. You can never "make" a child practice, but you can help to motivate. Listen to any frustrations or difficulties that your grandchild may have with motivation, practice technique, etc., and don't hesitate to discuss those with the teacher.
7. Practice daily—rather than just before the next lesson or the next concert.

What Is This Business about "Chairs"?

You'll undoubtedly hear about which "chair" your grandchild has been assigned in the ensemble. The child may be proud to make "first chair." This refers to the way young musicians are evaluated and which parts within the musical arrangement that they play. In some schools, chair assignments can be highly competitive, and one child may "challenge" another to obtain a higher chair. In other cases, the music teacher simply assigns the chairs after listening carefully to each music student. Either way works.

Some children don't react well to a competitive environment, whereas others thrive on it. One role for you as a grandparent is always to be encouraging regardless of the chair assigned to your grandchild. No matter which chair your grandchild achieves, each child is still making music with the group and each part remains vital for the success of the entire ensemble.

Festivals and Competitions

A good school system will participate in various music festivals and competitions, usually on an annual basis. For example, concert bands throughout the state may all assemble and perform separately. Each is **adjudicated**, that is, judged by a panel of accomplished conductors and provided with feedback and a rating about how well the group did.

Participation in and support of these competitions are useful to you as a grandparent, and if you can attend the competition, perhaps as a chaperone, do so! You'll hear a lot of other ensembles and be able to judge how well your grandchild's school system is doing in comparison to other schools around the state. Your attendance at the competition/festival will decidedly encourage your grandchild as well.

One form of competition is the Solo and Ensemble Festival. This kind of competition is especially useful for the improvement of musical performance. Small ensembles or a solo recital place demands on your grandchild that would never be experienced in a larger group. The music-making is much more intimate. Encourage your grandchild to participate in these opportunities.

Social Aspects of Musical Ensembles

One of the great benefits of participating in musical groups of all kinds is the social bonding that occurs, not only among the students and their peers, but also among the parents/grandparents of the child musicians. Both types of socialization are wonderful opportunities!

Although I attended high school more than 50 years ago, I still have friends from my high school band. They are lifelong connections. These are powerful friendships born from common experiences on life's journey. Participation in musical ensembles will give your grandchild a whole social circle of like-minded, conscientious students who want to do something artistically and who take great joy in the artistic experience. That alone is reason enough for you to encourage your grandchild to participate.

You can also develop a social network for yourself by getting to know other band parents and grandparents. Perhaps you could join the band boosters association. Band boosters help raise money to supplement an insufficient school music program budget. In joining them, you'll acquire a whole new set of friends from the community at large. That's good for you and for your grandchild.

Also, remember that your grandchild is likely to continue to make music as an adult, which provides opportunities for a rich social life in the future. The gift of music keeps on giving throughout a lifetime.

Purchasing a Professional-Quality Musical Instrument for Your Grandchild

If your grandchild shows dedication, conscientious persistence, and talent, it may be time to buy a better instrument, especially if the instrument is a flute, clarinet, saxophone, violin, or other instrument not supplied by the school system. Musical instruments are commonly manufactured at three levels:
1. Beginner or student models
2. Intermediate models
3. Professional models

While an intermediate model is an improvement over the beginner models, it is often possible to buy a used professional model that would be superior to a new intermediate level. Perhaps a professional player has one for sale in your area. Suggestions for finding a used professional instrument include:

- Talk to your local music store owner, who may have some used professional models in stock.
- Check craigslist, Facebook, or other online sources.
- Talk to your local community music school about instruments that have been donated.
- Talk to your grandchild's band or orchestra director to obtain further suggestions.

Always ask a professional player, perhaps your grandchild's private teacher, to play-test the instrument and appraise its value. You want to pay a fair price for the instrument but not overpay either.

The gift of a professional-quality instrument given to your conscientious, passionate, talented grandchild, if you can afford it, will always be cherished and will remind her of you forever. I still own a professional-model clarinet given to me by my maternal grandmother. While I now own many other instruments, that clarinet will always elicit special feelings for me. I strongly encourage you to purchase a professional-level instrument for your grandchild if it's at all possible for you financially.

Making Music a Career?

The life of a musician, whether instrumental artist or vocalist, is difficult and competitive. The reason? There are more musicians than the market can support at a reasonable income.

Success in the world of music depends on many attributes, but the two most important ones are diligence and talent. Diligence is even more important than talent. I've observed many highly talented musicians who simply didn't possess the necessary diligence to put in the many thousands of hours of practice required to achieve a high level of performance.

But children should follow their bliss, and if your grandchild is intent on a musical career, even after knowing the difficulties, I have some suggestions:

- A musician can always teach music as a primary career and perform professionally on the side.
- Your grandchild can take on another primary career—like accounting or even medicine–and perform semiprofessionally on the side.
- If intent on a professional career in music, the child can apply to a superb music school like Juilliard or Eastman School of Music. Admission would be a strong indication of talent.
- Always remember that these decisions are not irrevocable. If it doesn't work out, always have a fallback.
- Working in a field adjacent to music performance, such as a sound designer for films, a recording engineer, etc., is also an excellent option for your musical grandchild.

KEY POINTS

- The teen years are the time to make real music at a high level of proficiency.
- Many different types of ensembles can be formed in the school music program. Rock bands and garage bands are generally not taught formally, but many students find them fun.
- Practicing is essential. *Essential.* Encourage your grandchild but never nag. Praise but don't demand.
- Music can be competitive. As a grandparent, point out that making music with friends is the end point, not achieving a certain chair in the band.
- Good school systems send their vocal and instrumental ensembles to festivals and to competitions. This is a great opportunity to be a chaperone for the event!
- Music is largely a social activity. As the grandparent of a musical child, you can socialize with other band grandparents. Think about becoming a band booster!
- If you can possibly manage the finances, purchase a professional-quality instrument for your grandchild. A used instrument may be highly suitable. Make sure to ask a professional musician or your child's teacher to play-test the instrument prior to purchase.
- A career in music is a difficult choice, but it could still be the right one for your grandchild. Look for talent *and* diligence. Ask for advice. But also remember that no such decision is irrevocable. Encourage your grandchild to have a backup plan—a nonmusical profession that would be marketable, if needed.

Quick Summary of Key Points

Your Unique Role

- No one can replace the role of the grandparent in the musical (and general) development of grandchildren. Grandparents are more important than even they think they are!
- Your infant grandchild's brain is plastic: it grows and develops in response to stimuli such as music education.
- In the early years, expose your grandchild to as many different experiences as possible. Enrich your grandchild's environment.
- Learning is a game! Play musical games of all kinds.
- Music is a powerful enrichment because it involves virtually every part of your grandchild's brain.
- It doesn't matter at all if you're not a musician yourself. It only matters that you want to expose your grandchild to a variety of new experiences.
- In the early years of school, continue to be active with a variety of musical games.
- Think about starting your grandchild on piano or violin lessons at age four or five, realizing that they may not stay with that instrument.
- In the middle years of school, your grandchild will start lessons on various band and orchestra instruments. Encourage that!

- Your role during the teen years as a grandparent is no less important. Make certain that your grandchild has good instruction. Participate with band boosters. Purchase a professional-model instrument for your grandchild.

The **GUARANTEED** results of your efforts:
- Lifelong memories for you to share with your grandchild
- Close bonding with your grandchild
- A musically enriched life for your grandchild, probably leading to a better career and more satisfying interpersonal relationships

Appendix A:
Musical Toys in the Early Years

As infants grow into toddlers, various musical toys become invaluable for learning about music and for music-making. Fortunately, many are available at relatively low cost, and they tend to mimic ordinary musical instruments quite closely. In reality, anything that makes a sound could be considered a toy musical instrument. The physics of musical instruments are discussed in many books listed in the Further Reading section.

The Science of Musical Instruments

Physics dictates that all musical instruments have three requirements. They must have:

1. something that vibrates (the vibrator);
2. something to start the vibration (the driver); and
3. something to amplify the vibration (the resonator).

Musical instruments fall into four broad categories.

Instrument Type	Vibrator	Driver	Resonator
String	Strings	Bow or fingers	Hollow box
Brass	Buzzing lips	Breath	Brass tube
Woodwind	Reed	Breath	Wood or metal tube
Percussion	Body of instrument	Striker	Body of instrument

Examples of Toy Musical Instruments

String	Brass	Woodwind	Percussion
Plastic violin	Ask child to blow air through pierced lips to make a buzz sound	Recorder	Strike any object
Toy ukulele		Tonette	Toy drum
Simple lap harp		Harmonica	Juice harp
Single-string instrument		Whistle	Toy xylophone
		Drinking straw oboe*	

*The drinking straw oboe is a musical toy that you and your grandchild can make together, and it demonstrates a fundamental characteristic of woodwind instruments. Go to your kitchen and find some plastic drinking straws. Take a straw and pinch 2 or 3 cm (about an inch) of one end flat, or at least as flat as possible. Now, take scissors and cut the flattened end into a triangle about 1.5 cm (1/2 inch) long. The end of the straw thereby becomes the point of a triangle.

Take the cut triangle end of the straw, place it in your mouth, put your lips around the straw so that it's sealed, but don't apply so much pressure as to close off the flow of air through the straw. Blow through the straw in such a way that the triangle flaps begin to vibrate inside your mouth. This may require a few attempts to get it right.

Before long, you'll begin to hear a buzzing from the straw. You'll find that you can adjust the pitch of this buzzing in at least two ways: (1) by changing the position and pressure of your mouth on the straw, and (2) by changing the length of the straw by cutting it to shorter lengths with scissors. The shorter the straw, the higher the pitch will be. This simple drinking straw oboe demonstrates the key physical principles of woodwind instruments.

How Best to Learn with Musical Toys

Learning theorists have evidence that it's better to allow the toddler to explore the toy at first without any instruction whatsoever. Gradually, you, as the grandparent, can demonstrate some things to do with the toy. Be sure to ask questions at all stages of exploration:

- "How do you like that sound?"
- "What does it sound like?"
- "What if you hit it harder?"
- "What if you hit it softer?"
- "What if you do this at the same time as you do that?"

Exploration and self-discovery are valuable parts of play for your grandchild's developing young brain. Depending on your own musical background, you may actually end up discovering things together, and that could be an even better shared experience!

Appendix B:
Listening Activities for Young Ears

It almost goes without saying that listening to different types of music is an essential part of gaining full enjoyment from it. But what pieces? What purposes for each? Classical? Popular? Jazz? Rock? Ethnic music? Show tunes? Live performances? Recorded music?

The best answer? All of the above and even more!

Today, the availability of recorded music on various media is virtually unlimited. It becomes easy to fill your home with music as part of enriching the environment for your grandchildren.

As they grow into the toddler stage and beyond, you'll have the opportunity to teach your grandchild about listening to music and the tools that composers use to produce specific emotional responses. This Appendix is my attempt to give you, as a grandparent, some suggestions for music listening with your grandchild. It's by no means complete but will give you some ideas.

First off, let's define music. **Music** is sound organized against time. Key elements of music include melody, harmony, and rhythm. You can help your grandchild listen for all three of these. Composers also use a plethora of "tricks" to create emotional responses. They may use slower music to create a feeling of sadness or faster music to create happiness or energy. They may use softer music to create a feeling of transcendence and louder music to make us dance. They often change tempo and loudness throughout a piece of music.

Choose pieces of music that you yourself enjoy because your grandchild will sense your enjoyment. Over the course of your listening activities, you'll be able to help your grandchild investigate some of the following characteristics of music:

- Does slower music make you sad?
- Does faster music make you happy?
- What kind of music makes you want to dance?
- Can you sing along with this piece of music?
- What happens when two people sing together but aren't singing the same thing?
- How do you feel when you listen to a march?
- How do you feel when you listen to a hymn?
- Does this music make you want to sway?
- Would this music sound better to you if it were faster or slower? Louder or softer?
- How many different melodies can you count in this piece of music?
- Do you like music with singing or music with just instruments better?

The list of possible questions is endless, but that's enough to give you an idea. In my view, it does no one any good for you to introduce your grandchild to music that you definitely don't enjoy yourself. At the same time, you may want to "stretch" a bit and try to see the value in various kinds of ethnic or non-European music, especially Asian and African music, to give your grandchild a broader perspective. Don't forget to allow your grandchild to make choices as well and then discuss the reasons that the music is so appealing.

Listening to music with your grandchild is a bit like reading to the child. It's a rewarding, wonderful activity, especially when accompanied by question-and-answer conversation!

KEY POINTS

- Listen often to music of all kinds with your grandchild.
- Ask your grandchild to describe how the music makes her feel.
- Encourage your grandchild to choose the music.

Further Reading

Branscome, Eric. *Essential Listening Activities for the Music Classroom: Ready-to Use Lessons and Games for Grades Pre-K-8.* Van Nuys, Calif.: Alfred Music, 2008.

Cutietta, Robert A. *Raising Musical Kids: A Guide for Parents,* 2nd ed. New York: Oxford University Press, 2014.

Guarendi, Ray. *Being a Grandparent: Just Like Being a Parent…Only Different!* Cincinnati: Franciscan Media, 2018.

Healy, Jane M. *Your Child's Growing Mind: Brain Development and Learning from Birth to Adolescence,* 3rd ed. New York: Broadway Books, 2004.

James, Abel. *The Musical Brain.* BrainFood Productions, 2013.

Jourdain, Robert. *Music, the Brain, and Ecstasy: How Music Captures Our Imagination.* New York: HarperCollins Publishers, 1993.

Lithgow, John. *The Remarkable Farkle McBride.* New York: Simon & Schuster Books for Young Readers, 2000.

Montague, Michael J. *The Science of Music and the Music of Science: How Music Reveals Our Brain, Our Humanity, and the Cosmos.* St. Louis: Cosmic Music, LLC, 2019.

Patel, Aniruddh D. *Music, Language, and the Brain.* New York: Oxford University Press, 2008.

Powell, John. *How Music Works: The Science and Psychology of Beautiful Sounds, from Beethoven to the Beatles and Beyond.* New York: Little, Brown and Company, 2010.

Saunders, Laura I. *Your Brain on Music: The Cognitive Effects of Music Education on the Brain.* Higher Purpose Publishing, 2017.

Schaefer, Charles E., and Theresa Foy DiGeronimo. *Ages and Stages: A Parent's Guide to Normal Childhood Development.* New York: John Wiley & Sons, Inc., 2000.

Storms, Jerry. *101 Music Games for Children: Fun and Learning with Rhythm and Song.* Alameda, Calif.: Hunter House Inc., Publishers, 1995.

About the Author

Michael J. Montague earned his Ph.D. in cellular and molecular biology from The University of Michigan in 1974. Following post-doctoral studies at Stanford University, Dr. Montague began a 40-year research career with several major corporations, working on both the improvement of agricultural productivity and in pharmaceutical discovery, and additionally as a research manager, science communicator, and lecturer. During his career, he has enjoyed the immense privilege of membership on teams of research scientists who made major contributions that now benefit billions of people globally. At the same time, he worked as a card-carrying union musician, most often in the evenings, performing a wide variety of types of music, as well as arranging and composing. He has studied performance and music theory intensively with several excellent symphony musicians and teachers at Webster University in St. Louis and is most grateful for that valuable instruction. In addition, he has published original research on the acoustics of woodwind instruments.

Made in the USA
Monee, IL
01 June 2021